SHAKESPEARE'S
GUIDE
TO LIFE

Also by Michael Macrone
Brush Up Your Shakespeare
It's Greek to Me
By Jove!
Brush Up Your Bible
Eureka!
Animalogies

SHAKESPEARE'S GUIDE TO LIFE

*Truly Timeless Wisdom
from the Plays and Sonnets*

Edited by
MICHAEL MACRONE

HarperCollins*Publishers*

HarperCollins*Publishers*
77–85 Fulham Palace Road,
Hammersmith, London W6 8JB

Published by HarperCollins*Publishers* 1997
1 3 5 7 9 8 6 4 2

First published in the USA by
Crown Publishers Inc,1996

Copyright © Cader Company Inc, and Michael Macrone 1996

A catalogue record for this book is
available from the British Library

ISBN 0 00 638860 4

Set in Centaur

Printed and bound in Great Britain by
Scotprint Ltd, Musselburgh

Contents

SHAKESPEARE'S GUIDE TO LIFE

Introduction

Shakespeare's characters love to talk, and they're full of opinions on life. From Iago's "Put money in thy purse" (*Othello*) to Hamlet's "To be, or not to be" (*Hamlet*), from the mundane to the metaphysical, his plays and poems offer hundreds of observations and instructions on living, dying, loving, hating, acting, speaking, swearing, lying, buying, lending, dressing, drinking, and even cooking.

The catch is that Shakespeare doesn't tell us which instructions to follow.

The late Professor Joel Fineman of Berkeley once said that if Shakespeare's sonnets are written in the first and second persons, from an "I" to a "you," then his plays are written in the "zeroth" person—that is, from nobody. Romantic poet John Keats made essentially the same point in a famous letter of 1817, referring to the dramatist's "Negative Capability"—his ability to negate his own beliefs, his own self, in order to present characters and events without sentiment or personal coloring.

His characters' manner of speaking, their thoughts, opinions and attitudes, their temperaments and emotions, are proper to them, not to Shakespeare, whose own "voice" is elusive at best.

Not that Shakespeare's attitudes are a complete mystery. Sometimes what a character says is clearly ridiculous, sometimes clearly profound. But such cases are relatively rare, and it's impossible to add them up into some sort of Shakespearean philosophy.

All this makes compiling a book of Shakespeare's "advice" rather interesting. Inevitably the reader will, like the author, wonder if a given speech is serious or just rhetorical, whether the words are words to live by or to reject. The best answer in most cases is that there's really no way of separating the serious from the rhetorical, since by its very nature dramatic speech is *always* rhetorical, always dependent on the speaker's particular position and function in the play. (Shakespeare's are the *only* plays people seek through for philosophy.) If you ask whether Shakespeare himself believed what he wrote, the best answer is "maybe."

For example, Polonius in *Hamlet* is a tedious, pompous old man whose advice is stuffed full of Eliza-

than commonplaces. But does that mean Shakespeare, ho makes Polonius tedious, is mocking the advice? oes that make it wrong?

Likewise, the character Falstaff (in two histories and a omedy) is a coward, a braggart, and a rogue. On the ther hand, he's a lovable rogue, full of life and refresh- gly earthy. What, then, are we to make of his advice nd opinions? It's unlikely Shakespeare intended anyone follow Falstaff's advice and "addict themselves to ick" (see page 44): this is just Falstaff's being Falstaff.

But even when Falstaff's just being Falstaff—and hus being not entirely serious—he sometimes does peak a kind of truth. "What is honor?" he asks rhetor- :ally. "A word" (page 78). Of course honor is really lore than that, but Falstaff makes a good point: honor s as much an *idea* as a *thing*, if not more. His truth is artial, but in Shakespeare's hands, so are almost all ruths. Shakespeare, Keats said, was "capable of being n uncertainties, Mysteries, doubts, without any irritable eaching after fact & reason." In short, searching hrough the Bard's work (even the sonnets) for unam- iguous, "serious" advice is bound to fail. Whether the idvice applies, or the belief is true, all depends.

So why this book? Because even Shakespeare's am‑
biguous or rhetorical lessons make up a formidable an‑
thought-provoking catalogue, valuable as much for it‑
"Mystery" and contradictions as for its frequent clarit‑
and beauty. And whether Shakespeare is revealing hi‑
own thoughts, merely characterizing, quoting contem‑
porary attitudes, or exploring the many facets of truth
he stamps something of himself on the thoughts in th‑
act of composing his unique poetry and prose.

Like many quotation books, this one is divided int‑
topical chapters. The categories are somewhat fluid an‑
overlapping, but they do cluster together relate‑
thoughts on common experiences, from money trouble‑
to marital relations. (A few misfit quotations are col‑
lected in the chapter "General Instructions.")

In the back you will find explanatory notes, providin‑
exact citations, identifying the speakers and addressees
and glossing the quotations. Sometimes I merely "trans‑
late" Shakespeare's English, but more often I attempt t‑
briefly explain the context or the thought behind it. A‑
the very least, the notes make it easy to quiz Shake‑
speare-loving friends (or test yourself) on who sai‑
what, to whom, and where.

Act/scene/line numbers, lineation, and spelling (with a few modifications) follow the text of *The Riverside Shakespeare* (Houghton Mifflin, 1974). I frequently referred to the *Riverside* notes as well as to the commentary in the various volumes of *The Arden Shakespeare*. Also useful were other compilations of Shakespearean wisdom, especially G. F. Lamb's *Shakespeare Quotations* (Larousse, 1994) and *A Dictionary of Quotations from Shakespeare*, edited by Margaret Miner and Hugh Rawson (Signet, 1994).

MICHAEL MACRONE

Commerce & Coin

1.
Thrift, thrift, Horatio.

2.
Neither a borrower nor a lender be.

3.
If thou wilt lend this money, lend it not
As to thy friends, for when did friendship take
A breed for barren metal of his friend?
But lend it rather to thine enemy,
Who if he break, thou mayst with better face
Exact the penalty.

4.

He is well paid that is well satisfied.

5.

Poor and content is rich, and rich enough;
But riches fineless is as poor as winter
To him that ever fears he shall be poor.

6.

He that is robb'd, not wanting what is stol'n,
Let him not know't and he's not robb'd at all.

7.

'Tis very pregnant,
The jewel that we find, we stoop and take't
Because we see it; but what we do not see
We tread upon, and never think of it.

8.

Our basest beggars
Are in the poorest things superfluous.
Allow not nature more than nature needs,
Man's life is cheap as beast's.

9.

Distribution should undo excess
And each man have enough.

10.

He that wants money, means, and content is without
three good friends.

11.

Let me have no lying. It becomes none but tradesmen.

12.

Great business must be wrought ere noon.

13.

Sell when you can.

14.

Put money in thy purse.

15.

There is money, spend it, spend it; spend more;
spend all I have.

16.

Beauty provoketh thieves sooner than gold.

17.

The learned pate
Ducks to the golden fool.

18.

How quickly nature falls into revolt
When gold becomes her object!

19.

All gold and silver rather turn to dirt.

20.

What's aught but as 'tis valued?

21.

Nothing comes amiss, so money comes withal.

Men & Women

22.

Sigh no more, ladies, sigh no more,
Men were deceivers ever,
One foot in sea and one on shore,
To one thing constant never.

23.

'Tis not a year or two shows us a man:
They are all but stomachs, and we all but food;
They eat us hungerly, and when they are full
They belch us.

24.

I wonder men dare trust themselves with men.

25.

The chariest maid is prodigal enough
If she unmask her beauty to the moon.

26.

If ladies be but young and fair,
They have the gift to know it.

27.

*There was never yet fair woman
but she made mouths in a glass.*

28.

Frailty, thy name is woman!

29.

A woman mov'd is like a fountain troubled,
Muddy, ill-seeming, thick, bereft of beauty,
And while it is so, none so dry or thirsty
Will deign to sip, or touch one drop of it.

30.

*Make the doors upon a woman's wit, and it will
out at the casement; shut that, and 'twill out at the
key-hole; stop that, 'twill fly with the smoke out
at the chimney.*

31.

Two women plac'd together makes cold weather.

32.

Were kisses all the joys in bed,
One woman would another wed.

33.

Women are angels wooing:
Things won are done, joy's soul lies in the doing.
That she belov'd knows nought that knows not this:
Men prize the thing ungain'd more than it is.

34.

Win her with gifts, if she respects not words:
Dumb jewels often in their silent kind
More than quick words do move a woman's mind.

35.

Let thy love be younger than thyself,
Or thy affection cannot hold the bent;
For women are as roses, whose fair flow'r
Being once display'd, doth fall that very hour.

36.

Fair flowers that are not gath'red in their prime
Rot, and consume themselves in little time.

37.

He that hath no beard is less than a man.

38.

Those girls of Italy, take heed of them.
They say our French lack language to deny
If they demand.

Love

39.

If music be the food of love, play on.

40.

Give me some music; music, moody food
Of us that trade in love.

41.

What is love? 'Tis not hereafter;
Present mirth hath present laughter;
What's to come is still unsure.
In delay there lies no plenty,
Then come kiss me sweet and twenty;
Youth's a stuff will not endure.

42.

Never durst poet touch a pen to write
Until his ink were temp'red with Love's sighs.

43.

You must lay lime to tangle her desires
By wailful sonnets.

44.

Love goes toward love as schoolboys from their books,
But love from love, toward school with heavy looks.

45.

Love is a smoke made with the fume of sighs.

46.

The hind that would be mated by the lion
Must die for love.

47.

Men have died from time to time, and worms have eaten them, but not for love.

48.

To be wise and love
Exceeds man's might; that dwells with gods above.

49.

Love is blind, and lovers cannot see
The pretty follies that themselves commit.

50.

Love is too young to know what conscience is.

51.

Who ever lov'd that lov'd not at first sight?

52.

The course of true love never did run smooth.

53.

What love can do, that dares love attempt.

54.

Love may transform me to an oyster.

55.

Love moderately: long love doth so;
Too swift arrives as tardy as too slow.

56.

Lovers ever run before the clock.

57.

When love begins to sicken and decay
It useth an enforced ceremony.

58.

The love of wicked men converts to fear,
That fear to hate, and hate turns one or both
To worthy danger and deserved death.

59.

Lovers and madmen have such seething brains,
Such shaping fantasies, that apprehend
More than cool reason ever comprehends.

60.

By heaven, I do love, and it hath taught me to rhyme
and to be melancholy.

61.

These fellows of infinite tongue, that can rhyme
themselves into ladies' favors, they do always reason
themselves out again.

62.

O absence, what a torment wouldst thou prove,
 Were it not thy sour leisure gave sweet leave
To entertain the time with thoughts of love.

63.

Love that comes too late,
 Like a remorseful pardon slowly carried,
To the great sender turns a sour offence,
 Crying, "That's good that's gone."

64.

Hope is a lover's staff; walk hence with that
And manage it against despairing thoughts.

65.

There's beggary in the love that can be reckon'd.

66.

Base men being in love have then a nobility in their
natures more than is native to them.

67.

Black men are pearls in beauteous ladies' eyes.

68.

Love knows it is a greater grief
To bear love's wrong than hate's known injury.

69.

Love is merely a madness, and I tell you, deserves as
well a dark house and a whip as madmen do.

70.

I had rather hear my dog bark at a crow
than a man swear he loves me.

Jealousy & Hate

71.
Love, thou know'st, is full of jealousy.

72.
O, beware, my lord, of jealousy.
It is the green-ey'd monster which doth mock
The meat it feeds on.

73.
How many fond fools serve mad jealousy!

74.

I had rather be a toad
And live upon the vapor of a dungeon
Than keep a corner in the thing I love
For others' uses.

75.

So full of artless jealousy is guilt,
It spills itself in fearing to be spilt.

76.

Jealous souls will not be answer'd so;
They are not ever jealous for the cause
But jealous for they're jealous.

77.

The venom clamors of a jealous woman
Poisons more deadly than a mad dog's tooth.

78.

Never anger
Made good guard for itself.

79.

Anger is like
A full hot horse, who being allow'd his way,
Self-mettle tires him.

80.

Men that make
Envy and crooked malice nourishment
Dare bite the best.

81.

In time we hate that which we often fear.

Passion & Lust

82.

Th' expense of spirit in a waste of shame
Is lust in action.

83.

Love comforteth like sunshine after rain,
But Lust's effect is tempest after sun;
Love's gentle spring doth always fresh remain,
Lust's winter comes ere summer half be done.

84.

Violent fires soon burn out themselves;
Small show'rs last long, but sudden storms are short.

85.

Let every eye negotiate for itself,
And trust no agent; for beauty is a witch
Against whose charms faith melteth into blood.

86.

Keep you in the rear of your affection,
Out of the shot and danger of desire.

87.

Rebellious hell,
If thou canst mutine in a matron's bones,
To flaming youth let virtue be as wax
And melt in her own fire.

88.

The power of beauty will sooner transform honesty
from what it is to a bawd than the force of honesty can
translate beauty into his likeness.

89.

But virtue, as it never will be moved,
Though lewdness court it in a shape of heaven,
So lust, though to a radiant angel link'd,
Will sate itself in a celestial bed
And prey on garbage.

90.

*Hot blood begets hot thoughts, and hot thoughts
beget hot deeds, and hot deeds is love.*

91.

'Tis the strumpet's plague
To beguile many and be beguil'd by one.

92.

Lechery, lechery, still wars and lechery, nothing else
holds fashion.

93.

It is a bawdy planet.

Marriage & Family

94.

Let me not to the marriage of true minds
Admit impediments.

95.

A young man married is a man that's marr'd.

96.

Hanging and wiving goes by destiny.

97.

She's not well married that lives married long,
But she's best married that dies married young.

98.

The instances that second marriage move
Are base respects of thrift, but none of love.

99.

Get thee a good husband, and use him as he uses thee

100.

Thou wilt never get thee a husband, if thou be so
shrewd of thy tongue.

101.

Hasty marriage seldom proveth well.

102.

Time goes on crutches till love have all his rites.

103.

Get thee to a nunn'ry.

104.

Loss of virginity is rational increase, and there was never virgin got till virginity was first lost.

105.

To speak on the part of virginity is to accuse your mothers, which is most infallible disobedience. He that hangs himself is a virgin; virginity murthers itself, and should be buried in highways out of all sanctified limit, as a desperate offendress against nature. Virginity breeds mites, much like a cheese, consumes itself to the very paring, and so dies with feeding his own stomach.

106.

Besides, virginity is peevish, proud, idle, made of self-love, which is the most inhibited sin in the canon.

107.

Men are merriest when they are from home.

108.

Women are so simple
To offer war where they should kneel for peace,
Or seek for rule, supremacy, and sway,
When they are bound to serve, love, and obey.

109.

A light wife doth make a heavy husband.

110.

Should all despair
That have revolted wives, the tenth of mankind
Would hang themselves.

111.

Take thou no scorn to wear the horn. . . .
The horn, the horn, the lusty horn,
Is not a thing to laugh to scorn.

112.

I do think it is their husbands' faults
If wives do fall.

113.

It is a wise father that knows his own child.

114.

'Tis a happy thing
To be father unto many sons.

115.

How sharper than a serpent's tooth it is
To have a thankless child!

116.

A decrepit father takes delight
To see his active child do deeds of youth.

117.

If I had a thousand sons, the first human principle
I would teach them should be, to forswear thin
potations and to addict themselves to sack.

Pleasure & Pain

118.

Let the world slip, we shall ne'er be younger.

119.

Frame your mind to mirth and merriment,
Which bars a thousand harms and lengthens life.

120.

There was never yet philosopher
That could endure the toothache patiently.

121.

He that sleeps feels not the toothache.

122.
He jests at scars that never felt a wound.

123.
Mirth cannot move a soul in agony.

124.
The worst is not
So long as we can say, "This is the worst."

125.
Hope to joy is little less in joy
Than hope enjoyed.

126.
Silence is the perfectest herald of joy; I were but little
happy, if I could say how much.

127.
Sweets grown common lose their dear delight.

128.

Sweet are the uses of adversity.

129.

The labor we delight in physics pain.

130.

In poison there is physic.

131.

All delights are vain, but that most vain
Which, with pain purchas'd, doth inherit pain.

132.

Misery acquaints a man with strange bedfellows.

133.

O, how bitter a thing it is to look into happiness
through another man's eyes!

Judgment & Law

134.

***In the course of justice, none of us
Should see salvation.***

135.

The gods are just, and of our pleasant vices
Make instruments to plague us.

136.

Forbear to judge, for we are sinners all.

137.

Use every man after his desert, and who shall
scape whipping?

138.
The quality of mercy is not strain'd.

139.
Nothing emboldens sin so much as mercy.

140.
We must not make a scarecrow of the law,
Setting it up to fear the birds of prey,
And let it keep one shape, till custom make it
Their perch and not their terror.

141.

Thieves for their robbery have authority
When judges steal themselves.

142.
Change places, and handy-dandy, which is the justice,
which is the thief?

143.
A dog's obey'd in office.

144.
The brain may devise laws for the blood, but a hot temper leaps o'er a cold decree.

145.
The most peaceable way for you, if you do take a thief, is to let him show himself what he is, and steal out of your company.

146.
Every subject's duty is the King's, but every subject's soul is his own.

147.
The first thing we do, let's kill all the lawyers.

Wit & Wisdom

148.
Ignorance is the curse of God,
Knowledge the wing wherewith we fly to heaven.

149.
There are more things in heaven and earth, Horatio,
Than are dreamt of in your philosophy.

150.
Study is like the heaven's glorious sun,
That will not be deep search'd with saucy looks;
Small have continual plodders ever won,
Save base authority from others' books.

151.

There is occasions and causes why and wherefore in all things.

152.

Better a witty fool than a foolish wit.

153.

The fool doth think he is wise, but the wise man knows himself to be a fool.

154.

Cudgel thy brains no more about it, for your dull ass will not mend his pace with beating.

155.

I had rather a fool to make me merry than experience
to make me sad.

156.

I'll see before I doubt; when I doubt, prove.

157.

Thus may poor fools
Believe false teachers.

158.

Lord, what fools these mortals be!

159.

*I am a great eater of beef, and I believe that does
harm to my wit.*

Words & Deeds

160.

Talkers are no good doers.

161.

Men of few words are the best men.

162.

Brevity is the soul of wit.

163.

More matter with less art.

164.

Speak on, but be not over-tedious.

165.

Speak to me home, mince not the general tongue.

166.

Be check'd for silence,
But never tax'd for speech.

167.

Quietness, grown sick of rest, would purge
By any desperate change.

168.

Ill deeds is doubled with an evil word.

169.

Tell truth and shame the devil.

170.

An honest tale speeds best being plainly told.

171.

The truest poetry is the most feigning.

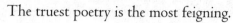

172.

Grant I may never grow so fond
To trust man on his oath or bond.

173.

'Tis not the many oaths that make the truth,
But the plain single vow that is vow'd true.

174.

It is a great sin to swear unto a sin,
But greater sin to keep a sinful oath.

175.

What fool is not so wise
To lose an oath to win a paradise?

176.

I will praise any man that will praise me.

177.

The worthiness of praise disdains his worth,
If that the prais'd himself bring the praise forth.

178.

He that is proud eats up himself. Pride is his
own glass, his own trumpet, his own chronicle,
and whatever praises itself but in the deed,
devours the deed in the praise.

179.

Suit the action to the word, the word to the action,
with this special observance, that you o'erstep not
the modesty of nature: for any thing so o'erdone is
from the purpose of playing, whose end, both at the
first and now, was and is, to hold as 'twere the mirror
up to nature: to show virtue her feature, scorn her
own image, and the very age and body of the time
his form and pressure.

180.

Let those that play your clowns speak no more than is
set down for them.

181.
Very good orators, when they are out, they will spit.

Action

182.
O heavens, what some men do,
While some men leave to do!

183.
If ever fearful
To do a thing, where I the issue doubted,
Whereof the execution did cry out
Against the non-performance, 'twas a fear
Which oft infects the wisest.

184.

We must not stint
Our necessary actions in the fear
To cope malicious censurers, which ever,
As rav'nous fishes, do a vessel follow
That is new trimm'd, but benefit no further
Than vainly longing.

185.

Our doubts are traitors,
And makes us lose the good we oft might win,
By fearing to attempt.

186.

The sleeping and the dead
Are as but pictures; 'tis the eye of childhood
That fears a painted devil.

187.

In the night, imagining some fear,
How easy is a bush suppos'd a bear!

188.

Many will swoon when they do look on blood.

189.

Screw your courage to the sticking place.

190.

If it were done, when 'tis done, then 'twere well
It were done quickly.

191.

What's done cannot be undone.

192.

Between the acting of a dreadful thing
And the first motion, all the interim is
Like a phantasma or a hideous dream.

193.

Thus conscience doth make cowards of us all
And thus the native hue of resolution
Is sicklied o'er with the pale cast of thought.

194.

When our actions do not,
Our fears do make us traitors.

195.

Foul deeds will rise,
Though all the earth o'erwhelm them, to men's eyes.

196.

Things done well
And with a care exempt themselves from fear;
Things done without example, in their issue
Are to be fear'd.

197.

If to do were as easy as to know what were good to do,
chapels had been churches, and poor men's cottages
princes' palaces.

Honesty & Hypocrisy

198.

To be honest, as this world goes, is to be one man
pick'd out of ten thousand.

199.

Men should be what they seem.

200.

One may smile, and smile, and be a villain!

201.

There's daggers in men's smiles.

202.

What may man within him hide,
Though angel on the outward side!

203.

The dev'l hath power
T' assume a pleasing shape.

204.

The devil can cite Scripture for his purpose.

205.

Take note, take note, O world,
To be direct and honest is not safe.

206.

Be not thy tongue thy own shame's orator;
Look sweet, speak fair, become disloyalty.

207.

Honesty coupled to beauty is to have honey a
sauce to sugar.

208.

If I tell thee a lie, spit in my face, call me horse.

209.

Falsehood falsehood cures.

210.

False face must hide what the false heart doth know.

211.

Time shall unfold what plaited cunning hides.

212.

*What a fool Honesty is! and Trust, his sworn
brother, a very simple gentleman!*

213.

To show an unfelt sorrow is an office
Which the false man does easy.

214.

Do not, as some ungracious pastors do,
Show me the steep and thorny way to heaven,
Whiles, like a puff'd and reckless libertine,
Himself the primrose path of dalliance treads,
And reaks not his own rede.

215.

Things are often spoke and seldom meant.

Virtues & Vices

216.
The better part of valor is discretion.

217.
Assume a virtue, if you have it not.

218.
*There is nothing either good or bad, but thinking
makes it so.*

219.
Evils that take leave,
On their departure most of all show evil.

220.

The art of our necessities is strange
And can make vile things precious.

221.

There is no virtue like necessity.

222.

The devil Luxury [has a] fat rump and potato finger.

223.

The evil that men do lives after them,
The good is oft interred with their bones.

224.

Men's evil manners live in brass, their virtues
We write in water.

225.

Blest are those
Whose blood and judgment are so well co-meddled,
That they are not a pipe for Fortune's finger
To sound what stop she please.

226.

How far that little candle throws his beams!
So shines a good deed in a naughty world.

227.

Heaven doth with us as we with torches do,
Not light them for themselves.

228.

Is it a world to hide virtues in?

229.

Nought so vile that on the earth doth live
But to the earth some special good doth give.

230.

There is some soul of goodness in things evil,
Would men observingly distil it out.

231.

A good heart, Kate, is the sun and the moon, or
rather the sun and not the moon; for it shines bright
and never changes, but keeps his course truly.

232.

A heart unspotted is not easily daunted.

233.

Virtue is bold, and goodness never fearful.

234.

True nobility is exempt from fear.

235.

When valor preys on reason,
It eats the sword it fights with.

236.

What valor were it, when a cur doth grin,
For one to thrust his hand between his teeth
When he might spurn him with his foot away?

237.

*I never knew yet but rebuke and check was the
reward of valor.*

238.

Virtue finds no friends.

239.

Virtue is beauty, but the beauteous evil
Are empty trunks o'er-flourish'd by the devil.

240.

In nature there's no blemish but the mind;
None can be call'd deform'd but the unkind.

241.

'Tis the mind that makes the body rich;
And as the sun breaks through the darkest clouds,
So honor peereth in the meanest habit.

242.

There is no vice so simple but assumes
Some mark of virtue on his outward parts.

243.

Virtue itself turns vice, being misapplied,
And vice sometime's by action dignified.

244.

Some rise by sin, and some by virtue fall.

245.

If sack and sugar be a fault, God help the wicked!

246.

He's truly valiant that can wisely suffer
The worst that man can breathe, and make his wrongs
His outsides, to wear them like his raiment, carelessly,
And ne'er prefer his injuries to his heart,
To bring it into danger.

247.

The robb'd that smiles steals something from the thief;
He robs himself that spends a bootless grief.

248.

Bid that welcome
Which comes to punish us, and we punish it
Seeming to bear it lightly.

249.

Rightly to be great
Is not to stir without great argument,
But greatly to find quarrel in a straw
When honor's at the stake.

250.

Who steals my purse steals trash; 'tis something, nothing; 'Twas mine, 'tis his, and has been slave to thousands; But he that filches from me my good name Robs me of that which not enriches him, And makes me poor indeed.

251.

The purest treasure mortal times afford
Is spotless reputation. . . .
Mine honor is my life, both grow in one;
Take honor from me, and my life is done.

252.

What is honor? A word.

Greatness & Ambition

253.

Greatness knows itself.

254.

Great men may jest with saints; 'tis wit in them,
But in the less foul profanation.

255.

Lowliness is young ambition's ladder,
Whereto the climber upward turns his face;
But when he once attains the upmost round,
He then unto the ladder turns his back,
Looks in the clouds, scorning the base degrees
By which he did ascend.

256.

Man, proud man,
Dress'd in a little brief authority,
Most ignorant of what he's most assur'd,
(His glassy essence), like an angry ape
Play such fantastic tricks before high heaven
As makes the angels weep.

257.

Th' abuse of greatness is when it disjoins
Remorse from power.

258.

Some are born great, some achieve greatness,
and some have greatness thrust upon 'em.

259.

Fortune brings in some boats that are not steer'd.

260.

Bootless speed
When cowardice pursues and valor flies.

261.

Celerity is never more admir'd
Than by the negligent.

262.

*It is the bright day that brings forth the adder,
And that craves wary walking.*

263.

'Tis time to fear when tyrants seems to kiss.

264.

Two stars keep not their motion in one sphere.

265.

Thriftless ambition . . . will raven up
Thine own life's means.

266.

'Tis the curse of service;
Preferment goes by letter and affection,
And not by old gradation.

267.

When beggars die there are no comets seen;
The heavens themselves blaze forth the death of
princes.

268.

'Tis better to be lowly born
And range with humble livers in content
Than to be perked up in a glist'ring grief
And wear a golden sorrow.

269.

Uneasy lies the head that wears a crown.

270.

Kingdoms are clay; our dungy earth alike
Feeds beast as man.

271.

Take physic, pomp,
Expose thyself to feel what wretches feel.

272.

They that stand high have many blasts to shake them,
And if they fall, they dash themselves to pieces.

273.

Men shut their doors against a setting sun.

274.

The great man down, you mark his favorite flies,
The poor advanc'd makes friends of enemies.
And hitherto doth love on fortune tend,
For who not needs shall never lack a friend,
And who in want a hollow friend doth try,
Directly seasons him his enemy.

275.

He that stands upon a slipp'ry place
Makes nice of no vile hold to stay him up.

276.

Our remedies oft in ourselves do lie,
Which we ascribe to heaven.

277.

Men at some time are masters of their fates;
The fault, dear Brutus, is not in our stars,
But in ourselves, that we are underlings.

278.

It is the stars,
The stars above us, govern our conditions,
Else one same mate and make could not beget
Such different issues.

279.

There is a tide in the affairs of men,
Which taken at the flood, leads on to fortune;
Omitted, all the voyage of their life
Is bound in shallows and in miseries.

280.

When Fortune means to men most good,
She looks upon them with a threat'ning eye.

281.

This is the state of man: to-day he puts forth
The tender leaves of hopes, to-morrow blossoms,
And bears his blushing honors thick upon him;
The third day comes a frost, a killing frost,
And when he thinks, good easy man, full surely
His greatness is a-ripening, nips his root,
And then falls as I do.

282.

Treason is but trusted like the fox,
Who never so tame, so cherish'd and lock'd up,
Will have a wild trick of his ancestors.

283.

Yond Cassius has a lean and hungry look,
He thinks too much; such men are dangerous.

Self & Society

284.

To thine own self be true.

285.

Love thyself last, cherish those hearts that hate thee.

286.

Be to yourself
As you would to your friend.

287.

Self-love, my liege, is not so vile a sin
As self-neglecting.

288.

Nature teaches beasts to know their friends.

289.

Those friends thou hast, and their adoption tried,
Grapple them to thy soul with hoops of steel,
But do not dull thy palm with entertainment
Of each new-hatch'd, unfledg'd courage.

290.

Those you make friends
And give your hearts to, when they once perceive
The least rub in your fortunes, fall away
Like water from ye, never found again
But where they mean to sink ye.

291.

To the noble mind
Rich gifts wax poor when givers prove unkind.

292.

To weep with them that weep doth ease some deal,
But sorrow flouted at is double death.

293.

Beware
Of entrance to a quarrel, but being in,
Bear't that th' opposed may beware of thee.

294.

Slander lives upon succession,
For ever hous'd where it gets possession.

295.

I am I, howe'er I was begot.

296.

We, ignorant of ourselves,
Beg often our own harms, which the wise pow'rs
Deny us for our good.

297.

To willful men,
The injuries that they themselves procure
Must be their schoolmasters.

298.

Therein the patient
Must minister to himself.

299.

Man, how dearly ever parted,
How much in having, or without or in,
Cannot make boast to have that which he hath,
Nor feels what he owes, but by reflection.

300.
One touch of nature makes the whole world kin.

301.

Things in motion sooner catch the eye
Than what stirs not.

302.

Time hath, my lord, a wallet at his back,
Wherein he puts alms for oblivion,
A great-siz'd monster of ingratitudes.

303.

Opinion's but a fool, that makes us scan
The outward habit for the inward man.

304.

Apparel oft proclaims the man.

305.
Small cheer and great welcome makes a merry feast.

306.
Society is no comfort
To one not sociable.

307.
Unbidden guests
Are often welcomest when they are gone.

Life & Death

308.

All the world's a stage,
And all the men and women merely players;
They have their exits and their entrances,
And one man in his time plays many parts.

309.

Life's but a walking shadow, a poor player,
That struts and frets his hour upon the stage,
And then is heard no more. It is a tale
Told by an idiot, full of sound and fury,
Signifying nothing.

310.

Life is as tedious as a twice-told tale
Vexing the dull ear of a drowsy man.

311.

*The web of our life is of mingled yarn, good
and ill together.*

312.

To be, or not to be, that is the question.

313.

It is great
To do that thing that ends all other deeds.

314.

Who would fardels bear,
To grunt and sweat under a weary life,
But that the dread of something after death,
The undiscover'd country, from whose bourn
No traveler returns, puzzles the will,
And makes us rather bear those ills we have,
Than fly to others that we know not of?

315.

The weariest and most loathed worldly life
That age, ache, penury, and imprisonment
Can lay on nature is a paradise
To what we fear of death.

316.

There is special providence in the fall of a sparrow.

317.

There's a divinity that shapes our ends,
Rough-hew them how we will.

318.

There is divinity in odd numbers, either in nativity,
chance, or death.

319.

Death, a necessary end,
Will come when it will come.

320.

Men must endure
Their going hence even as their coming hither:
Ripeness is all.

321.

This fell sergeant, Death,
Is strict in his arrest.

322.

Death, as the Psalmist saith, is certain to all,
all shall die.

323.

Golden lads and girls all must,
As chimney-sweepers, come to dust.

324.

Cowards die many times before their deaths,
The valiant never taste of death but once.

325.

The stroke of death is as a lover's pinch,
Which hurts, and is desir'd.

326.

I love long life better than figs.

327.

How many things by season season'd are
To their right praise and true perfection!

328.

The canker galls the infants of the spring
Too oft before their buttons be disclos'd,
And in the morn and liquid dew of youth
Contagious blastments are most imminent.

329.

How ill white hairs become a fool and jester!

330.

As they say, "When the age is in, the wit is out."

331.

Beauty doth vanish age, as if new born.

332.

Care keeps his watch in every old man's eye,
And where care lodges, sleep will never lie;
But where unbruised youth with unstuff'd brain
Doth couch his limbs, there golden sleep doth reign.

333.

Death's a great disguiser.

334.

'Tis a vile thing to die, my gracious lord,
When men are unprepar'd and look not for it.

335.

He that dies pays all debts.

336.

Praising what is lost
Makes the remembrance dear.

337.

If a man do not erect in this age his own tomb
ere he dies, he shall live no longer in monument
than the bell rings and the widow weeps.

338.

There's hope a great man's memory may outlive his life half a year.

339.

Time's the king of men,
He's both their parent, and he is their grave,
And gives then what he will, not what they crave.

340.

Time, that takes survey of all the world,
Must have a stop.

341.

As flies to wanton boys are we to th' gods,
They kill us for their sport.

342.

Lord, we know what we are, but know not what
we may be.

343.

*We are such stuff
As dreams are made on; and our little life
Is rounded with a sleep.*

General Instructions

344.

Beware the ides of March.

345.

Make a short shrift.

346.

'Tis an ill cook that cannot lick his own fingers.

347.

In cases of defence 'tis best to weigh
The enemy more mighty than he seems.

348.

Sweets with sweet war not, joy delights in joy.

349.

There's small choice in rotten apples.

350.

Lilies that fester smell far worse than weeds.

351.

Good reasons must of force give place to better.

352.

To mourn a mischief that is past and gone
Is the next way to draw new mischief on.

353.

A little fire is quickly trodden out,
Which being suffer'd, rivers cannot quench.

354.

Home-keeping youth have ever homely wits.

355.

Weariness
Can snore upon the flint, when resty sloth
Finds the down pillow hard.

356.

Fashion wears out more apparel than the man.

357.

Thus the whirligig of time brings in his revenges.

358.

What's in a name? That which we call a rose
By any other word would smell as sweet.

359.

The crow doth sing as sweetly as the lark
When neither is attended.

360.

The man that hath no music in himself,
Nor is not moved with concord of sweet sounds,
Is fit for treasons, stratagems, and spoils.

361.

Diseased nature oftentimes breaks forth
In strange eruptions.

362.

They laugh that wins.

363.

What a piece of work is a man, how noble in reason,
how infinite in faculties, in form and moving, how
express and admirable in action, how like an angel in
apprehension, how like a god! the beauty of the world;
the paragon of animals; and yet to me what is this
quintessence of dust?

364.

Some men there are love not a gaping pig;
Some that are mad if they behold a cat;
And others, when the bagpipe sings i' th' nose,
Cannot contain their urine.

365.

Ay, leeks is good.

Notes

Act, scene, and line numbers, as well as punctuation and spelling (occasionally modified), are those of *The Riverside Shakespeare*. The names of the speaker and, where there is one, the addressee are given in parentheses after the citation.

1. *Hamlet* I.ii.180 (Hamlet to Horatio)
   Usually quoted straight, this phrase is actually Hamlet's sarcastic appraisal of why his mother so hastily remarried after his father's death: the funeral baked meats could be served cold at the wedding banquet.

2. *Hamlet* I.iii.75 (Polonius to Laertes)
   Polonius means with friends, as you're apt to lose both them *and* the cash.

3. *The Merchant of Venice* I.iii.132 (Antonio to Shylock)
   Shylock questions whether he ought to lend money to Antonio, who doesn't like him at all; Antonio replies that if you're going to charge interest or penalize default, it's *better* to lend to enemies than to friends.

4. *The Merchant of Venice* IV.i.415
   (Portia to Antonio and Bassanio)
   If doing someone a service gives you satisfaction, that's all the payment you need.

5. *Othello* III.iii.172 (Iago to Othello)
   Poverty and wealth are states of mind: a little is enough if it contents you, while even boundless (*fineless*) wealth is poor if you're always afraid of losing it.

6. *Othello* III.iii.342 (Othello to Iago)
   What you don't know won't hurt you.

7. *Measure for Measure* II.i.23 (Angelo to Escalus)
   You can't be tempted by an unperceived lure. Though the plot revolves around a premature pregnancy, what Angelo means by *pregnant* is "obvious," the word's original sense.

8. *King Lear* II.iv.264 (Lear to Regan)
   If we didn't enjoy more than what we merely "need," our lives would be no better than an animal's.

9. *King Lear* IV.i.70 (Gloucester to Edgar)
   The Earl of Gloucester, having seen how the other half suffers, becomes a socialist. (The same has already happened to Lear: see #271)

10. *As You Like It* III.ii.24 (Corin to Touchstone)
    A shepherd's commonsense philosophy: If you lack (*want*) cash, employment, and happiness, you're hurting.

11. *The Winter's Tale* IV.iv.722 (Autolycus to Clown)
    Since Autolycus is a thief masquerading as a soldier, this line is straight irony. On the other hand, he probably *does* think thieves are at least as honest as tradesmen.

12. *Macbeth* III.v.22 (Hecate)
    Actually, the witch Hecate is only talking about noon the
    next day, by which time she and her cohorts will have had
    some "business" with Macbeth. But it's a good piece of
    advice anyway.

13. *As You Like It* III.v.60 (Rosalind to Phebe)
    Rosalind admonishes a vain shepherdess to think twice
    before rejecting marriage proposals—she may be pricing
    herself out of the market.

14. *Othello* I.iii.339 (Iago to Roderigo)
    Iago's self-serving advice to his dupe, whose money fre-
    quently takes a quick detour into Iago's own purse.

15. *The Merry Wives of Windsor* II.ii.231 (Ford to Falstaff)
    This is what jealousy has reduced Ford to: throwing
    money at the prodigal Falstaff.

16. *As You Like It* I.iii.110 (Rosalind to Celia)
    Travel is more dangerous if you're beautiful than if you're
    rich.

17. *Timon of Athens* IV.iii.17 (Timon)
    Even geniuses will toady to rich idiots.

18. *Henry IV, Part 2* IV.v.65 (King Henry IV)
    Believing his son covets the crown and wishes him dead,
    King Henry opines that kinship (*nature*) means nothing
    when wealth is at stake.

19. *Cymbeline* III.vi.53 (Arviragus to Imogen)
Therefore gold and silver oughtn't be coveted.

20. *Troilus and Cressida* II.ii.52 (Troilus to Hector)
What something's worth has nothing to do with what it
is, but only with what people *think* it's worth.

21. *The Taming of the Shrew* I.ii.81 (Grumio to Hortensio)
Anything's bearable if it makes you rich.

22. *Much Ado about Nothing* II.iii.62 (Balthasar, singing)
Men have been inconstant in love since the beginning of
time.

23. *Othello* III.iv.103 (Emilia to Desdemona)
Some welcome comic relief after Othello has first dis-
played his horrible jealousy.

24. *Timon of Athens* I.ii.43 (Apemantus to Timon)
Only a fool trusts other people.

25. *Hamlet* I.iii.36 (Laertes to Ophelia)
A modest (*chary*) girl will expose her flesh to no one except the moon. (*Prodigal* here means "immodest.")

26. *As You Like It* II.vii.37 (Jaques, quoting Touchstone)
A cynic observes that comely young women tend also to
be narcissistic.

27. *King Lear* III.ii.35 (Fool to Lear)
Beauty is vanity. Pretty women practice faces in their mir-
rors (*glasses*).

28. *Hamlet* I.ii.146 (Hamlet)
    Women (e.g., Hamlet's mother) are weak creatures.

29. *The Taming of the Shrew* V.ii.142 (Katherina)
    Women ought to be docile, or they'll never catch a husband.

30. *As You Like It* IV.i.161 (Rosalind to Orlando)
    If you're looking for peace and quiet, forget about living with a woman.

31. *Henry VIII* I.iv.22 (Lord Chamberlain to ladies)
    Women shouldn't sit side by side at a dinner party; the company's "warmer" if the sexes alternate.

32. *The Passionate Pilgrim*, xviii.47
    That Shakespeare wrote this verse is questionable.

33. *Troilus and Cressida* I.ii.286 (Cressida)
    Men think women divine while pursuing them; but having achieved their goal, they rapidly lose interest. Put another way, men overvalue what they wish for and undervalue what they have.

34. *The Two Gentlemen of Verona* III.i.89 (Valentine to Duke)
    If words fail, give diamonds a try.

35. *Twelfth Night* II.iv.36 (Duke Orsino)
    A man's love lasts only as long as a woman's beauty, which isn't very long.

36. "Venus and Adonis," line 131.
    Go for it while you're young and beautiful.

37. *Much Ado about Nothing* II.i.37 (Beatrice to Leonato)
    Don't worry: having to shave counts too.

38. *All's Well That Ends Well* II.i.19
    (King of France to young lords)
    Timeless advice—not just for Frenchmen, either.

39. *Twelfth Night* I.i.1 (Duke Orsino to Musicians)
    Music hath charms to gorge the lovesick stomach. The
    Duke romantically renounces romance: he wants to be so
    full of it that he gets sick.

40. *Antony and Cleopatra* II.v.1 (Cleopatra)
    A rewrite of Orsino's line (#39). This time there's no
    talk of sickening, but Cleopatra does call music *moody
    food*, that is, sad stuff.

41. *Twelfth Night* II.iii.48 (Feste, singing)
    Had we but world enough and time, this coyness, lady,
    were no crime.

42. *Love's Labour's Lost* IV.iii.343 (Berowne)
    In the course of "proving" that love rightly conquers all,
    Berowne claims that love is what inspires all true poetry.

43. *The Two Gentlemen of Verona* III.ii.68 (Proteus to Thurio)
    The surest way to snare a woman's heart is to write her
    desperate love poems. (*Lime* is a sticky bark extract used
    to trap birds.)

44. *Romeo and Juliet* II.ii.156 (Romeo)
    Romeo's response after Juliet has bid him "A thousand

times good night." Not an especially romantic metaphor, but then Romeo is but a lad.

45. *Romeo and Juliet* I.i.190 (Romeo to Benvolio)
    The lament of a frustrated lover: however bright and solid it seems at first, love is soon revealed to be dark and insubstantial, feeding on its victim's pains (thus *sighs*).

46. *All's Well That Ends Well* I.i.91 (Helena)
    If you aim beyond your sphere in love, be prepared to suffer for it.

47. *As You Like It* IV.i.101 (Rosalind to Orlando)
    Talk of "dying of heartbreak" is just that: talk. Science has never recorded a case of it.

48. *Troilus and Cressida* III.ii.156 (Cressida to Troilus)
    If a man is acting rationally and discreetly, he can't be in love, since lovers are by definition out of their minds.

49. *The Merchant of Venice* II.vi.36 (Jessica to Lorenzo)
    Lovers are blind not only to their loved one's faults, but to their own many follies as well. Jessica also means that we often do things for love that would be embarrassing otherwise.

50. Sonnet 151, line 1
    Love, like a child, is innocent and incapable of guilt. By the same token, it is also incapable of reason or morality.

51. *As You Like It* III.v.82 (Phebe)
    Coming from someone who's just fallen in love at first

sight, this is a rhetorical question. Phebe is quoting from Christopher Marlowe's racy unfinished poem "Hero and Leander" (ca. 1593).

52. *A Midsummer Night's Dream* I.i.134 (Lysander to Hermia)
Don't expect love to be all smooth sailing, especially when a playwright needs a few good comic plot twists.

53. *Romeo and Juliet* II.ii.68 (Romeo to Juliet)
Romeo's *can* means something more like "wills," so his point is that a lover will *attempt* to foil whatever obstacles love presents.

54. *Much Ado about Nothing* II.iii.24 (Benedick)
A constant theme in Shakespeare: Love can make you unrecognizable even to yourself. In this case, turning Benedick into *an oyster* (that is, "clamming him up") is a special feat, since he's such a loudmouth.

55. *Romeo and Juliet* II.vi.14 (Friar Lawrence to Romeo)
The immoderate acts of impassioned lovers are as apt to fail as the too-cautious acts of the timorous. In this case the friar is all too correct.

56. *The Merchant of Venice* II.vi.4 (Gratiano to Salerio)
In pursuit of love, lovers are seldom tardy.

57. *Julius Caesar* IV.ii.20 (Brutus to Lucilius)
Increasing formality is a sure sign of a dying friendship.

58. *Richard II* V.i.66 (King Richard to Northumberland)
    Abetting a villain will get you nowhere; instead of gratitude, you can expect only suspicion and danger.

59. *A Midsummer Night's Dream* V.4 (Theseus to Hippolyta)
    Lovers, like madmen, have a hard time telling reality apart from their fantasies. (Later in the speech, Theseus includes poets in the mix.)

60. *Love's Labour's Lost* IV.iii.12 (Berowne)
    The least sentimental of men are not immune to the power of love, which transforms them into melancholy poets.

61. *Henry V* V.ii.154 (King Henry to Princess Katherine)
    The poetic suitor soon becomes the rational cad.

62. Sonnet 39, line 9
    Separation from a lover is awful, but it does leave plenty of time for pondering love.

63. *All's Well That Ends Well* V.iii.57 (King of France to Bertram)
    Hard verses to follow, even in context. The king's basic point is that we often don't appreciate what we have till it's gone, and then we make loud noises about losing it.

64. *The Two Gentlemen of Verona* III.i.248 (Proteus to Valentine)
    When love seems thwarted, you must use hope to fend off despair.

65. *Antony and Cleopatra* I.i.14 (Antony to Cleopatra)
    If you can say how much you're in love, you're not.

66. *Othello* II.i.215 (Iago to Roderigo)
    Love induces noble feelings (like courage) even in an ill-bred man. Iago is referring to Roderigo, and thus insults him.

67. *The Two Gentlemen of Verona* V.ii.12 (Proteus to Thurio)
    A curious old saying meaning that beautiful women have a taste for ugly men. (In this context *black* means "dark, swarthy.")

68. Sonnet 40, line 11
    You expect your enemies to hurt you; a lover's injury, being unexpected, hurts worse.

69. *As You Like It* III.ii.400 (Rosalind to Orlando)
    I'm not sure if this was more funny or less when they actually dealt with madmen that way.

70. *Much Ado about Nothing* I.i.131 (Beatrice to Benedick)
    Tip: When a Shakespearean character says something like this, you can bet he or she will be in love by Act IV.

71. *The Two Gentlemen of Verona* II.iv.177 (Valentine to Proteus)
    True love means always fearing the loss of your lover.

72. *Othello* III.iii.165 (Iago to Othello)
    Jealousy eats you up and makes a fool of you. Iago should know; he's the one driving Othello mad.

73. *The Comedy of Errors* II.i.116 (Luciana to Adriana)
    Jealousy is a stupid waste of time. *Fond* is a synonym of *foolish*.

74. *Othello* III.iii.270 (Othello)
    A characteristically colorful comparison that shows what
    Othello thinks of adultery. The "toad" metaphor also in-
    dicates how thoroughly he's bought into Iago's mind-set.

75. *Hamlet* IV.v.19 (Gertrude)
    Two possible meanings: (1) The guilty, acting out of
    paranoia (*artless jealousy*), reveal their guilt despite them-
    selves; (2) Fear of the consequences will ruin (*spill*) a
    guilty man just as effectively as the consequences them-
    selves.

76. *Othello* III.iv.159 (Emilia to Desdemona)
    It's not enough to tell a man he has no cause to be *jealious*
    (an alternative spelling). For once a man is jealous, the
    power of his feeling outstrips any cause or reason. To the
    jealous mind, nothing can ever be proved.

77. *The Comedy of Errors* V.i.69
    (Lady Abbess to Adriana)
    A jealous woman's biting attacks are enough to drive a
    man mad.

78. *Antony and Cleopatra* IV.i.9 (Maecenas to Caesar)
    An angry man is a careless man.

79. *Henry VIII* I.i.132 (Norfolk to Buckingham)
    If you give anger full rein, it will soon exhaust itself.

80. *Henry VIII* V.ii.78 (Cranmer)
    Even the best men may be accused of evil, for greatness
    feeds envy.

81. *Antony and Cleopatra* I.iii.12 (Charmian to Cleopatra)
Be careful of whom you threaten, and how often.

82. Sonnet 129, line 1
To act on lust is to waste your energy on something you'll regret.

83. "Venus and Adonis," line 799 (Adonis to Venus)
While true love is ever fresh and gentle, lust is violent, tempestuous, and brief.

84. *Richard II* II.i.34 (John of Gaunt to Duke of York)
Passions and immoderate enthusiasms quickly "burn out" their victims, while moderate feelings are long and steady.

85. *Much Ado about Nothing* II.i.178 (Claudio)
Don't trust a friend to help you win a beautiful lover, for beauty is bewitching and liable to prompt him to woo for himself.

86. *Hamlet* I.iii.34 (Laertes to Ophelia)
Laertes, taking after his father Polonius, issues his sister stingy instructions. Applying a military metaphor, he advises Ophelia to check her feelings for Hamlet, whom Laertes considers dangerous.

87. *Hamlet* III.iv.82 (Hamlet to Gertrude)
If someone middle-aged (like Gertrude) can't resist lust, what hope is there for the young?

88. *Hamlet* III.i.110 (Hamlet to Ophelia)
A beautiful woman will sooner succumb to tempta-
tion and lose her *honesty* (chastity) than her honesty
will dull her beauty's naughty charms. The second half
of this quip is pretty thick, existing mostly to balance
the conceit.

89. *Hamlet* I.v.53 (Ghost to Hamlet)
Virtue cannot be overcome by lust, even if tempted by a
heavenly-seeming creature. Lust, on the other hand,
grows bored even with the favors of an angel.

90. *Troilus and Cressida* III.i.129 (Paris to Helen)
A witty and cynical observation typical of this play; for
hot understand "lusty."

91. *Othello* IV.i.96 (Iago)
A whore, whose loveless charms ensnare dozens of men,
will inevitably fall for one of them.

92. *Troilus and Cressida* V.ii.192 (Thersites)
Everything else may come and go, but there's always sex
and war.

93. *The Winter's Tale* I.ii.201 (Leontes to Mamillius)
Actually, this isn't a general comment on mortal lust;
what Leontes means is that adultery (*it*) is as inevitable
and ruinous as the ill effects of a malignant star. (In
those days people blamed all sorts of things on planetary
influences.)

94. Sonnet 116, line 1
    You've found a soul mate if your love can overcome all
    obstacles.

95. *All's Well That Ends Well* II.iii.298 (Parolles to Bertram)
    A proverbial pun: marriage is ruin, so it's best postponing
    it. (*Married* and *marred* sounded more alike then.)

96. *The Merchant of Venice* II.ix.83 (Nerissa to Portia)
    Some fates are inescapable, no matter how hard you try.

97. *Romeo and Juliet* IV.v.77 (Friar Lawrence to Capulet)
    Not so much a comment on marriage (though that too)
    as the friar's awkward attempt to calm Juliet's family after
    her seeming death. The general theme of his speech is
    that you shouldn't weep for the dead if you know they've
    gone to heaven.

98. *Hamlet* III.ii.182 (Player Queen to Player King)
    The usual reason for remarriage is money, not love. Ham-
    let's attack on his mother, veiled within a courtly enter-
    tainment.

99. *All's Well That Ends Well* I.i.214 (Parolles to Helena)
    Parolles is not a character whose advice is usually trust-
    worthy, so this statement is probably ironic. The verb *use*
    often connotes "abuse."

100. *Much Ado about Nothing* II.i.18 (Leonato to Beatrice)
    Shrewd means "shrewish," which really means "aggressive."

101. *Henry VI, Part 3* IV.i.18 (Richard to King Edward)
Richard may be evil, but in this case he's got a point.

102. *Much Ado about Nothing* II.i.357 (Claudio to Don Pedro)
If you've saved it for marriage, your wedding day can seem a *long* time coming.

103. *Hamlet* III.i.120 (Hamlet to Ophelia)
Hamlet recommends celibacy to his girlfriend, as having children is "breeding sinners."

104. *All's Well That Ends Well* I.i.127 (Parolles to Helena)
One of Parolles's many arguments against virginity. Even if you think virginity is so great a virtue, no virgin is ever born without a woman's losing that virtue.

105. *All's Well That Ends Well* I.i.136 (Parolles to Helena)
Parolles continues: Virginity, far from being noble, is actually a sin against nature, for it spells the extinction of your line and is thus tantamount to suicide. Besides, to celebrate virginity is to insult your own mother.

106. *All's Well That Ends Well* I.i.143 (Parolles to Helena)
What's more, virginity is a form of pride (of putting yourself before other people), which is condemned over and over in the Bible.

107. *Henry V* I.ii.272 (King Henry to French Ambassador)
What Henry really means by *merry* is "apt to misbehave."

108. *The Taming of the Shrew* V.ii.151
(Katherina to Bianca and Widow)
The former shrew gives lessons on proper feminine submission.

109. *The Merchant of Venice* V.i.130 (Portia to Bassanio)
Not a comment on relative poundage, but a pun on *light* in the sense "loose, wanton."

110. *The Winter's Tale* I.ii.198 (Leontes)
Revolted means "unfaithful." Leontes is so mad with jealousy that one wonders why he chooses so conservative a percentage.

111. *As You Like It* IV.ii.13 (group song)
In Shakespeare, *horn* almost always alludes to the "cuckold's horn," which symbolically adorns the unlucky husband's forehead. According to this tune, a man should not be ashamed to wear the horn, for it was worn by his father and grandfather before him.

112. *Othello* IV.iii.86 (Emilia)
If a woman is unfaithful, it's because her husband's own behavior drove her to it.

113. *The Merchant of Venice* II.ii.76
(Launcelot Gobbo to Old Gobbo)
The clown Gobbo inverts an old proverb: "It is a wise child that knows his own father." The original (let alone Gobbo's version) might not seem all that "wise," but in those days men were extra paranoid about adultery.

114. *Henry VI, Part 3* III.ii.104 (King Edward to Lady Grey)
     In this case the king refers to the preexisting offspring of
     the lady he hopes to marry.

115. *King Lear* I.iv.288 (Lear)
     Lear is an authority on this, as he's begotten two snakes
     in Goneril and Regan.

116. Sonnet 37, line 1
     We delight in seeing our children do what we no longer
     can.

117. *Henry IV, Part 2* IV.iii.122 (Falstaff)
     Real men drink sherry (*sack*), not thin stuff like beer.

118. *The Taming of the Shrew* Induction.ii.142
     (Christopher Sly to Page)
     An amalgam of old sayings, which add up to "Ignore
     your cares and have fun while you can; you're not getting
     any younger."

119. *The Taming of the Shrew* Induction.ii.135 (Messenger to Sly)
     Comedy is therapeutic, laughter being the best medicine.

120. *Much Ado about Nothing* V.i.35 (Leonato to Antonio)
     Intellectuals like to prattle about the virtues of stoic
     endurance, but only until they're actually in pain.
     Benedick, also complaining of a toothache, has already
     put it more plainly: "Everyone can master a grief but he
     that hath it" (III.ii.28).

121. *Cymbeline* V.iv.172 (First Jailer to Posthumus)
    I'm beginning to wonder if Shakespeare ever flossed.

122. *Romeo and Juliet* II.ii.1 (Romeo)
    Metaphorical: he who laughs at the lover's agonies must
    never have felt them himself. But before long Romeo will
    be feeling some literal wounds.

123. *Love's Labour's Lost* V.ii.857 (Berowne to Rosaline)
    If you think you're so funny, try joking with someone in
    pain and misery.

124. *King Lear* IV.i.27 (Edgar)
    If you can say "This is the worst," then at least you're still
    alive; and even if it's true (this side of death), logically
    things can only get better.

125. *Richard II* II.iii.15 (Northumberland to Bullingbrook)
    The anticipation can be as sweet as the achievement.

126. *Much Ado about Nothing* II.i.306 (Claudio to Beatrice)
    True joy cannot be measured or expressed in words;
    speechlessness is its sign.

127. Sonnet 102, line 12
    Scarcity makes pleasures sweeter; familiarity breeds con-
    tempt.

128. *As You Like It* II.i.12 (Duke Senior)
    Given a lemon, you might as well make lemonade.

129. *Macbeth* II.iii.50 (Macbeth to Macduff)
When hard work is fulfilling, it's no longer laborious. (In Macbeth's case, this is merely an ironic pleasantry.)

130. *Henry IV, Part 2* I.i.137 (Northumberland)
Even the worst news may have positive effects (*physic* means "medicine" or "healing"). The earl seeks a silver lining in the dark cloud of his son Hotspur's death.

131. *Love's Labour's Lost* I.i.72 (Berowne to King)
Sneer all you like at pleasure-seeking; it's still more sensible than suffering for something (like knowledge) that makes you unhappy in the end.

132. *The Tempest* II.ii.39 (Trinculo)
A jester's profound observation: adversity has a habit of forcing you to make common cause with people you'd rather avoid.

133. *As You Like It* V.ii.43 (Orlando to Rosalind)
It's hard to be happy for anyone, even your own brother, if he gets something you can't have.

134. *The Merchant of Venice* IV.i.198 (Portia to Shylock)
If God were as rigid a judge as some people, we'd all be damned to hellfire.

135. *King Lear* V.iii.171 (Edgar to Edmund)
Our sins, however pleasant at the time, often have unpleasant consequences. (Edgar refers to Gloucester's adultery, which produced Edmund the bastard, whose cronies put out Gloucester's eyes.)

136. *Henry VI, Part 2* III.iii.31 (King Henry to Warwick)
    Don't be so fast to see the evil in others; first take stock of
    your own.

137. *Hamlet* II.ii.529 (Hamlet to Polonius)
    We're all of us sinners. More concrete than Portia's similar line at *The Merchant of Venice* IV.i.198 (#134).

138. *The Merchant of Venice* IV.i.184 (Portia to Shylock)
    True mercy is wholly voluntary; one cannot be forced
    into it.

139. *Timon of Athens* III.v.3 (First Senator to Second Senator)
    You thought the Athenians were democrats, but really
    they were proto-Republicans.

140. *Measure for Measure* II.i.1 (Angelo to Escalus)
    Laws meant to deter crime won't work if you don't enforce them.

141. *Measure for Measure* II.ii.175 (Angelo)
    By *authority* Angelo literally means "precedent," but he implies "excuse."

142. *King Lear* IV.vi.153 (Lear to Gloucester)
    Put a judge in a thief's shoes, and the thief in the judge's,
    and soon it will be hard to tell who's the thief. That is,
    people tend to be treated according to their roles, and
    then to live up to them. (*Handy-dandy*, a children's game,
    here means "take your pick.")

143. *King Lear* IV.vi.158 (Lear to Gloucester)
Put the most worthless person in a position of authority, and everyone bows.

144. *The Merchant of Venice* I.ii.18 (Portia to Nerissa)
Passion is stronger than reason.

145. *Much Ado about Nothing* III.iii.57 (Dogberry to watchmen)
The constable Dogberry explains how to be a true keeper of the peace.

146. *Henry V* IV.i.176 (King Henry, disguised, to soldiers)
In more modern terms, you can't blame your own bad work on the boss.

147. *Henry VI, Part 2* IV.ii.76 (Dick to Jack Cade)
Shakespeare knew this was a surefire crowd-pleaser.

148. *Henry VI, Part 2* IV.vii.73 (Lord Say to Jack Cade)
Knowledge brings us closer to God, therefore its absence is a curse.

149. *Hamlet* I.v.166 (Hamlet to Horatio)
Just because you went to a hotshot university doesn't mean you know everything.

150. *Love's Labour's Lost* I.i.84 (Berowne to King)
Too much study gains you little besides a brain full of other people's opinions—better to respectfully avert your eyes. (*Saucy* means "impertinent," leading to the 18th-century put-down *saucebox*.)

151. *Henry V* V.i.3 (Fluellen to Gower)
There's an explanation for everything, no matter how strange. (*Why* and *wherefore* are nearly synonyms, but the fomer signifies "from what cause," while the latter means "for what purpose.")

152. *Twelfth Night* I.v.36 (Feste)
It's far better to have the wit to know you're a fool than to mistake yourself for a wit.

153. *As You Like It* V.i.31 (Touchstone, quoting, to William)
A very old saying, which goes back to Socrates at least.

154. *Hamlet* V.i.56 (First Clown to Second Clown)
A gravedigger's witty comment on his companion's lack of wit: A dull mind is like a lethargic beast of burden—it won't work any better no matter how hard you beat it.

155. *As You Like It* IV.i.27 (Rosalind to Jaques)
Happiness is good no matter how you come by it.

156. *Othello* III.iii.190 (Othello to Iago)
Don't believe anything until you've got a good reason to. (*Prove* means "test the truth.") Unfortunately, Othello is fooling himself.

157. *Cymbeline* III.iv.84 (Imogen to Pisanio)
Imogen blames herself for having believed in love letters.

158. *A Midsummer Night's Dream* III.ii.115 (Puck, singing)
Puck has a point, but he neglects to mention that the fools in question are under the influence of fairy dust.

159. *Twelfth Night* I.iii.85
     (Sir Andrew Aguecheek to Sir Toby Belch)
     Spoken by a fool, which may reflect Shakespeare's opinion of this contemporary dietary notion.

160. *Richard III* I.iii.350 (First Murderer to Richard)
     Never trust a loudmouth to follow through.

161. *Henry V* III.ii.36 (Boy)
     An old proverb and a recurring theme for Shakespeare, a man of many words. Loquacity is suspicious, a signal of evasion, vanity, or pretense.

162. *Hamlet* II.ii.90 (Polonius to Claudius and Gertrude)
     Getting right to the point is the essence of smart discourse. Unfortunately, Polonius rarely takes his own advice.

163. *Hamlet* II.ii.95 (Gertrude to Polonius)
     More content with less rhetoric.

164. *Henry VI, Part 1* III.iii.43 (Duke of Burgundy to Pucelle)
     I.e., "Make it snappy."

165. *Antony and Cleopatra* I.ii.105 (Antony to Messenger)
     Antony wants to know exactly what people are saying about him, without any *mincing* (softening). The *general tongue* is what we might now call the "buzz."

166. *All's Well That Ends Well* I.i.67 (Countess to Bertram)
     Parting advice from mother to son: It's better to be blamed for saying too little than for saying too much.

167. *Antony and Cleopatra* I.iii.53 (Antony to Cleopatra)
Disgruntled people quickly grow restless and are easily stirred into desperate actions.

168. *The Comedy of Errors* III.ii.20
(Luciana to Antipholus of Syracuse)
If you're deceiving someone (like your wife), it doubles the injury to flaunt it. Luciana really harps on this argument—see also #206.

169. *Henry IV, Part 1* III.i.58 (Hotspur to Owen Glendower)
A common proverb.

170. *Richard III* IV.iv.358 (Queen Elizabeth to King Richard)
If you're telling the truth, eloquence is more a hindrance than a help.

171. *As You Like It* III.iii.19 (Touchstone to Audrey)
Poets must *feign* or "lie" (spin fictions) in order to create "truth" (a higher view of life). This is Touchstone's account of why lovers tell lies, for "lovers are given to poetry."

172. *Timon of Athens* I.ii.64 (Apemantus)
Only a fool trusts other people.

173. *All's Well That Ends Well* IV.ii.21 (Diana to Bertram)
A sincere vow is worth more than dozens of insincere ones.

174. *Henry VI, Part 2* V.i.182 (Salisbury to King Henry)
No one should be bound to honor a pledge when doing so is sinful.

175. *Love's Labour's Lost* IV.iii.69
(Longaville, quoting his sonnet to Maria)
It's no sin to renege on a vow if one stands to gain "paradise"—in this case, the favors of a lovely lady. Longaville is, of course, rationalizing.

176. *Antony and Cleopatra* II.vi.88 (Enobarbus to Menas)
A frank admission of what most people do, sometimes called "logrolling."

177. *Troilus and Cressida* I.iii.241 (Aeneas to Agamemnon)
Nobody believes a braggart, even if he's telling the truth.

178. *Troilus and Cressida* II.iii.154 (Agamemnon to Ajax)
Agamemnon picks up where Aeneas left off (#177): Vanity only detracts from the good one is vain of.

179. *Hamlet* III.ii.17 (Hamlet to players)
A long way of saying that theater should closely imitate life.

180. *Hamlet* III.ii.38 (Hamlet to players)
Jokers tend to ham it up, which too often gets out of hand.

181. *As You Like It* IV.i.75 (Rosalind to Orlando)
When at a loss for words, do *something*—don't stand there speechless.

182. *Troilus and Cressida* III.iii.132 (Ulysses to Achilles)
If great men (like Achilles) don't do what needs to b
done, then fools (like Ajax) will, and will be applaude
for doing it.

183. *The Winter's Tale* I.ii.258 (Camillo to Leontes)
Even the wisest people sometimes fear the consequence
of their actions.

184. *Henry VIII* I.ii.76 (Wolsey to King Henry)
Fear of bad-mouthing shouldn't stop those in powe
from doing the right thing, especially since envious bad
mouthing is inevitable.

185. *Measure for Measure* I.iv.77 (Lucio to Isabella)
Fear of failure often leads us to despair of things w
might have achieved had we tried.

186. *Macbeth* II.ii.50 (Lady Macbeth to Macbeth)
Only children and weaklings are afraid of scary image
and dead things.

187. *A Midsummer Night's Dream* V.i.21 (Theseus to Hippolyta)
Theseus, unconsciously dangling a participle, conclude
his self-satisfied discourse on the overactive imagination
of poets, lovers, and lunatics.

188. *As You Like It* IV.iii.158 (Oliver to Celia)
Oliver's remarkable insight upon seeing Rosalind faint a
the sight of blood.

189. *Macbeth* I.vii.60 (Lady Macbeth to Macbeth)
    The lady wants Macbeth to stop acting like such a wimp and to just get on with killing Duncan. She doesn't explain what she means by *sticking place*, though.

190. *Macbeth* I.vii.1 (Macbeth)
    If acting will get something over with, it's best to act quickly. Unfortunately, most acts have consequences and are not *done* (ended) when they're *done* (performed).

191. *Macbeth* V.i.68 (Lady Macbeth)
    The impetuous lady realizes too late that she's not invulnerable to the consequences of her actions.

192. *Julius Caesar* II.i.63 (Brutus)
    The time between plotting an evil act and executing it is frightening and surreal, like a nightmare.

193. *Hamlet* III.i.82 (Hamlet)
    Thinking too much gets in the way of doing anything.

194. *Macbeth* IV.ii.3 (Lady Macduff to Rosse)
    Desperation as well as malice may lead us to treacherous deeds.

195. *Hamlet* I.ii.256 (Hamlet)
    Sooner or later an evil deed, no matter how well hid, will come to light.

196. *Henry VIII* I.ii.88 (King Henry to Wolsey)
    If you do something carefully, you needn't worry about

the outcome, which is only risky when the action has no
guide (*example*).

197. *The Merchant of Venice* I.ii.12 (Portia to Nerissa)
It's easier to preach than to practice, or to think than
to act.

198. *Hamlet* II.ii.178 (Hamlet to Polonius)
Hamlet counts himself among the few and includes
Polonius in the many.

199. *Othello* III.iii.126 (Iago to Othello)
Hypocrisy is naughty. Once again, Iago mouths honor-
able banalities that apply to no one so little as to himself.

200. *Hamlet* I.v.108 (Hamlet)
It's apparently news to Hamlet that bad guys are often
good actors, and that smiling faces sometimes pretend to
be your friend.

201. *Macbeth* II.iii.140 (Donalbain to Malcolm)
Not a general comment on smiling villains this time, but
only a remark about the folks at Macbeth's castle.

202. *Measure for Measure* III.ii.271 (Duke)
Appearances can be deceiving; devils may look like angels.

203. *Hamlet* II.ii.599 (Hamlet)
Who appears an angel (such as your father's ghost) may
turn out to be Satan.

204. *The Merchant of Venice* I.iii.98 (Antonio to Bassanio)
     A villain can twist anything to his purpose, even the
     Word of God.

205. *Othello* III.iii.377 (Iago to Othello)
     Honesty isn't always the best policy, since people have a
     habit of blaming the messenger. More rhetoric from the
     hypocrite Iago.

206. *The Comedy of Errors* III.ii.10
     (Luciana to Antipholus of Syracuse)
     If you're going to betray someone, at least have the heart
     not to show it.

207. *As You Like It* III.iii.29 (Touchstone to Audrey)
     It's great when a woman is beautiful; if not, she ought at
     least to be *honest* (chaste). But chastity in a beautiful
     woman is an excess of virtue.

208. *Henry IV, Part 1* II.iv.193 (Falstaff to Prince Henry)
     In Shakespeare's day calling someone a "horse" was
     rather insulting. Though Falstaff disavows lies, he's in
     the middle of telling a few big ones.

209. *King John* III.i.277 (Pandulph to King Philip)
     Two wrongs *do* make a right. More specifically, if you've
     sworn to something bad, it's better to break that oath
     than to keep it.

210. *Macbeth* I.vii.82 (Macbeth to Lady Macbeth)
If you're plotting something evil, make sure to hide it with a smiling face.

211. *King Lear* I.i.280 (Cordelia to Goneril and Regan)
Elaborate shams will in time be exposed. (*Plaited* means "pleated, intricately folded.")

212. *The Winter's Tale* IV.iv.595 (Autolycus)
Honest people have a difficult time telling when they're being hoodwinked.

213. *Macbeth* II.iii.136 (Malcolm to Donalbain)
Hypocrites are good at hypocrisy (specifically, shedding crocodile tears).

214. *Hamlet* I.iii.47 (Ophelia to Laertes)
Ophelia hopes her brother will practice what he preaches (*reak* his own *rede*) regarding sexual modesty. Incidentally, Ophelia coins *primrose path* in this speech.

215. *Henry VI, Part 2* III.i.268 (Suffolk to Queen Margaret)
Brave words are nice, but wait until they're executed before applauding.

216. *Henry IV, Part 1* V.iv.120 (Falstaff)
Honor isn't worth much once you're dead, and cowardice (*discretion*) can be a handy way to stay alive.

217. *Hamlet* III.iv.160 (Hamlet to Gertrude)
You should at least act virtuous even if you're not, since over time you'll get used to it.

218. *Hamlet* II.ii.249
   (Hamlet to Rosencrantz and Guildenstern)
   Hamlet: liberal humanist relativist.

219. *King John* III.iv.114 (Pandulph to Lewis the Dolphin)
   Things look worst right when they're about to get better.

220. *King Lear* III.ii.70 (Lear to Fool)
   Things we would normally despise can seem precious in
   distress. (The instant case is a straw-strewn hovel that
   shelters Lear from a raging storm.)

221. *Richard II* I.iii.278 (John of Gaunt to Bullingbrook)
   It's not what we *would* do that proves our virtue; it's what
   we *must* do. In other words, one should "make a virtue of
   necessity," making the best of every situation.

222. *Troilus and Cressida* V.ii.55 (Thersites)
   The salty Thersites wryly personifies lust (*luxury*); in
   Shakespeare's day, potatoes were considered aphrodisiacs.

223. *Julius Caesar* III.ii.75 (Antony to the plebeians)
   Once you're in the ground, people tend to forget your
   good side and remember only the bad.

224. *Henry VIII* IV.ii.45 (Griffith to Katherine)
   Griffith recycles Antony's more famous line (#223),
   adding a new metaphor: what is etched in brass is fixed,
   while water holds no shape.

225. *Hamlet* III.ii.68 (Hamlet to Horatio)
   Only those whose passion and intellect are perfectly

mixed (*meddled*) can resist the whims of Fortune (i.e., un-planned disasters).

226. *The Merchant of Venice* V.i.89 (Portia to Nerissa).
The darker a room, the more penetrating even a little light seems. Just so, the more wicked one's fellows, the more impressive one's good deeds, however small.

227. *Measure for Measure* I.i.32 (Duke to Angelo)
Our virtues are like a torch's flames, which God gave us to shine upon others—otherwise, we might as well not be virtuous.

228. *Twelfth Night* I.iii.131
(Sir Toby Belch to Sir Andrew Aguecheek)
Not if you actually have any—for what good is virtue if you don't make it known? However, Sir Andrew is a vain dolt and an abject coward.

229. *Romeo and Juliet* II.iii.17 (Friar Lawrence)
Nothing in nature, no matter how base or disgusting, is without *some* value. (No, the friar's poetry doesn't get better.)

230. *Henry V* IV.i.4 (King Henry to Bedford)
You can find the good in anything if you try hard enough.

231. *Henry V* V.ii.162 (King Henry to Princess Katherine)
Henry may not be handsome or eloquent, but he has a good heart, which will remain as strong, warm, and con-stant as the sun.

232. *Henry VI, Part 2* III.i.100 (Gloucester to Suffolk)
Those with a clear conscience fear no accusations (compare #233).

233. *Measure for Measure* III.i.208 (Duke to Isabella)
If you are truly good, you needn't fear any assault, for your virtue will carry you through it.

234. *Henry VI, Part 2* IV.i.129 (Suffolk to his captors)
Great men fear nothing other men can do.

235. *Antony and Cleopatra* III.xiii.198 (Enobarbus)
If courage leads you to irrational acts, it renders itself ineffectual.

236. *Henry VI, Part 3* I.iv.56 (Northumberland to Clifford)
Don't dignify the base acts of a villain by treating them more seriously than they deserve.

237. *Henry IV, Part 2* IV.iii.31 (Falstaff to Prince John)
No good deed goes unpunished, though Falstaff hasn't done one.

238. *Henry VIII* III.i.126
(Queen Katherine to Wolsey and Campeius)
The world is a wicked place; mere goodness earns you no points.

239. *Twelfth Night* III.iv.369 (Antonio to Viola)
Though goodness is beautiful, beauty is no guarantee of goodness. There are handsome villains, made comely not by nature but by the devil's art.

240. *Twelfth Night* III.iv.367 (Antonio to Viola)
Nothing in nature is ugly but the evil men do.

241. *The Taming of the Shrew* IV.iii.172 (Petruchio to Katherina)
You may wear ratty clothes, but if you have a noble mind it will shine through, all the brighter by contrast. (Petruchio may or may not buy his own advice, but he's in the middle of humiliating Kate.)

242. *The Merchant of Venice* III.ii.81 (Bassanio)
Simple means "pure, unalloyed"; and nothing in life is simple.

243. *Romeo and Juliet* II.iii.21 (Friar Lawrence)
Good intentions don't ensure good results; bad intentions sometimes lead to good.

244. *Measure for Measure* II.i.38 (Escalus)
Life can be unfair, rewarding the wicked and punishing the virtuous.

245. *Henry IV, Part 1* II.iv.470 (Falstaff to Prince Henry)
From one of Falstaff's many speeches defending liquor and sweets.

246. *Timon of Athens* III.v.31 (First Senator to Alcibiades)
It is not courageous to act on your anger, but rather to protect your spirit from the corroding forces of passion.

247. *Othello* I.iii.208 (Duke to Brabantio)
One of a string of smug couplets advising Desdemona's father to stop moaning about her marriage to Othello.

---

248. *Antony and Cleopatra* IV.xiv.136 (Antony to his men)
This might seem an odd thing for Antony to say after having just fallen on his sword, but it's simply more of the same Roman stoicism.

249. *Hamlet* IV.iv.53 (Hamlet)
Terrific poetry, but what Hamlet meant to say is "Rightly to be great/Is not *not* to stir without great argument [reason]. . . ." Except he doesn't mean *that* either; he's just ironically citing the common wisdom: namely, that "great" men get to be great by making a big deal out of meaningless quarrels and offenses to their honor.

250. *Othello* III.iii.157 (Iago to Othello)
Iago doesn't believe this for a minute, but he knows it sounds nice. The money in your wallet is a common thing, having been handled by many before you. Your reputation, on the other hand, is unique to you and thus more precious than such alienable stuff as cash. No one can "steal" your honor in the sense money can be stolen, for the thief doesn't earn a good reputation by taking yours away, nor can he simply give it back.

251. *Richard II* I.i.177 (Mowbray to King Richard)
An exemplary instance of the Renaissance madness for "honor," that is, reputation. Without it, Mowbray claims, life is worthless.

252. *Henry IV, Part 1* V.i.133 (Falstaff)
Falstaff rather disagrees with Mowbray: "Honor" is a

mere sign or appearance with no true substance. So why bother?

253. *Henry IV, Part 1* IV.iii.74 (Hotspur to Sir Walter Blunt)
Great men know they're great, which prompts them to aspire to power that is not always rightfully theirs.

254. *Measure for Measure* II.ii.127 (Isabella to Angelo)
"Important" people can get away with the worst faults just because they're important.

255. *Julius Caesar* II.i.22 (Brutus)
The ambitious man will act humble and ingratiating as a means of ascent; but having attained his goal he becomes haughty and dismissive. Further, once he's reached the top he'll want to pull the ladder up after him.

256. *Measure for Measure* II.ii.117 (Isabella to Angelo)
Power corrupts. Though temporary, authority makes men arrogant and prompts them to do naughty things that imperil what's permanent in them, namely their soul (*glassy essence*).

257. *Julius Caesar* II.i.18 (Brutus)
Power can go to your head and make you forget compassion.

258. *Twelfth Night* II.v.145 (Malvolio, quoting letter)
If, like Malvolio, you have neither the breeding nor the talent for greatness, don't despair—there's always luck. For example, a countess might fall in love with you.

259. *Cymbeline* IV.iii.46 (Pisanio)
Things often happen by chance, without anyone's planning them.

260. *A Midsummer Night's Dream* II.i.233 (Helena to Demetrius)
The literal sense of *bootless* is "futile," but Helena could be punning.

261. *Antony and Cleopatra* III.vii.24 (Cleopatra to Antony)
A cutting remark. Antony was marvelling at his enemies' speed and efficiency; Cleopatra sneers that they seem so fast only because Antony's moving so slow.

262. *Julius Caesar* II.i.14 (Brutus)
It's when a man assumes power that he becomes most dangerous, and then that others should tread most cautiously.

263. *Pericles* I.ii.79 (Pericles to Helicanus)
Or even when they just shake hands.

264. *Henry IV, Part 1* V.iv.65 (Prince Henry to Hotspur)
There's only room for one hotheaded golden boy per kingdom.

265. *Macbeth* II.iv.28 (Rosse to Macduff)
Ambition is an ingrate, devouring (*ravening up*) whatever gets in its way, including what once sustained it. (Rosse comments on allegations that King Duncan's two sons hired hit men to kill him.)

266. *Othello* I.i.35 (Iago to Roderigo)
When it comes to promotions, contacts and favoritism count for a lot more than seniority.

267. *Julius Caesar* II.ii.30 (Calphurnia to Caesar)
The heavenly powers couldn't care less about commoners, but they get pretty upset when great men die.

268. *Henry VIII* II.iii.19 (Anne Bullen to Old Lady)
The higher you climb, the harder you fall; better to never taste power and prestige than to have them and lose them.

269. *Henry IV, Part 2* III.i.31 (King Henry IV)
Kings have a lot to worry about, so you should feel sorry for them.

270. *Antony and Cleopatra* I.i.35 (Antony to Cleopatra)
Why get all worked up over property, which is just made of dirt?

271. *King Lear* III.iv.33 (Lear)
It would be good medicine (*physic*) for the rich to really know what it means to be poor.

272. *Richard III* I.iii.258
(Queen Margaret to Marquess of Dorset)
The high and mighty are targets for trouble, and they have a long way to fall.

273. *Timon of Athens* I.ii.145 (Apemantus)
     The cynic Apemantus's observation that friends will turn to strangers in your decline. This is indeed Timon's future.

274. *Hamlet* III.ii.204 (Player King to Player Queen)
     Friendship bows to fortune: observe the stampede of formerly flattering "friends" from a fallen star.

275. *King John* III.iv.137 (Pandulph to Lewis the Dolphin)
     Beggars can't be choosers: if you're in a tight spot, you'll accept help from anybody.

276. *All's Well That Ends Well* I.i.216 (Helena)
     If you want something, you have to try for it yourself and not count on heaven to intervene.

277. *Julius Caesar* I.ii.139 (Cassius to Brutus)
     We should blame ourselves, not fate, for failing in our ambitions.

278. *King Lear* IV.iii.32 (Kent to Gentleman)
     Kent means that some higher power, rather than birth, determines our characters. Otherwise, there's no explanation for how the same parents produced the saintly Cordelia and the satanic Regan and Goneril.

279. *Julius Caesar* IV.iii.218 (Brutus to Cassius)
     Seize the day; opportunities must be grasped when ripe, else life will be poor and miserable.

280. *King John* III.iv.119 (Pandulph to Lewis the Dolphin)
Good luck doesn't look so good at first.

281. *Henry VIII* III.ii.352 (Wolsey)
Wolsey blames his downfall on cold fate, which inevitably destroys those who achieve too much. Actually, though, it was his own fault.

282. *Henry IV, Part 1* V.ii.9 (Worcester to Vernon)
Once a villain, always a villain.

283. *Julius Caesar* I.ii.194 (Caesar to Antony)
So eat a lot and think a little.

284. *Hamlet* I.iii.78 (Polonius to Laertes)
Polonius doesn't mean "follow your bliss"; he means "put your own material interests first."

285. *Henry VIII* III.ii.443 (Wolsey to Cromwell)
True Christian advice from a man who didn't often heed it before being forced to eat a mighty slice of humble pie.

286. *Henry VIII* I.i.135 (Norfolk to Buckingham)
Try to view your problems and setbacks dispassionately, advising yourself as you would a friend in the same situation.

287. *Henry V* II.iv.74 (Dolphin to French King)
Better to be proud than a patsy; modesty is vulnerability. Wise words from the most self-loving character in the play.

288. *Coriolanus* II.i.6 (Sicinius to Menenius)
Even dumb animals know their friends from their enemies, and so do the masses.

289. *Hamlet* I.iii.62 (Polonius to Laertes)
Polonius throws a wet blanket over his paean to friendship: don't let the fun get out of hand.

290. *Henry VIII* II.i.127 (Buckingham)
Yet another variation on the theme of false friendship, re-
peated so often in Shakespeare that one has to wonder
about *his* friends.

291. *Hamlet* III.i.99 (Ophelia to Hamlet)
Gifts lose their charm when the giver does.

292. *Titus Andronicus* III.i.244 (Marcus)
It really hurts when someone mocks your calamities. And
believe me, there's more than enough calamity in this play
to go around.

293. *Hamlet* I.iii.65 (Polonius to Laertes)
Try not to get into fights, but if you do, act mean.

294. *The Comedy of Errors* III.i.105
(Balthazar to Antipholus of Ephesus)
Once people start gossiping about you there will never
be an end to it.

295. *King John* I.i.175 (Philip the Bastard to Queen Elinor)
Don't put too much stock in pedigree; a person's virtues
should speak for themselves.

296. *Antony and Cleopatra* II.i.5 (Menecrates to Pompey)
Sometimes it's better if we *don't* get what we want.

297. *King Lear* II.iv.302 (Regan to Gloucester)
Stubborn people have to learn from their own injuries, since they won't listen to others' advice.

298. *Macbeth* V.iii.45 (Doctor to Macbeth)
The only doctor for a diseased conscience is the self. Obviously, psychotherapy was not the fashion in Shakespeare's day.

299. *Troilus and Cressida* III.iii.96 (Ulysses to Achilles)
Ulysses chats philosophy with vain Achilles: You can neither know nor enjoy your virtues unless other people acknowledge them.

300. *Troilus and Cressida* III.iii.175 (Ulysses to Achilles)
Lest you find the sentiment sweet, Ulysses defines this *touch of nature* in the next quotation.

301. *Troilus and Cressida* III.iii.183 (Ulysses to Achilles)
What makes us all brethren is that we love what's new and flashy and ignore what's old and solid.

302. *Troilus and Cressida* III.iii.145 (Ulysses to Achilles)
People are forgetful ingrates. Ulysses pictures Time stuffing *alms* (good deeds) in a *wallet* (sack) for the monster *oblivion* (forgetfulness).

303. *Pericles* II.ii.56 (Simonides)
Popular opinion, which is foolish, values a man according to his looks; but virtues are often hidden.

304. *Hamlet* I.iii.72 (Polonius to Laertes)
What you wear says a lot about who you are.

305. *The Comedy of Errors* III.i.26
(Balthazar to Antipholus of Ephesus)
Good company is more important than good food.

306. *Cymbeline* IV.ii.12 (Imogen to Guiderius)
Some people are happiest left alone.

307. *Henry VI, Part 1* II.ii.55 (Bedford to Talbot)
No kidding.

308. *As You Like It* II.vii.139 (Jaques)
From a higher view, life appears as a trivial and formulaic fiction, in which you're just a stock figure playing a series of roles. Shakespeare gave this Elizabethan commonplace a dry run in *The Merchant of Venice*, where Antonio calls the world "a stage, where every man must play a part" (I.i.78)

309. *Macbeth* V.v.24 (Macbeth)
Macbeth, having lost everything including his better self, concludes that life is an empty, meaningless drama.

310. *King John* III.iv.108 (Lewis the Dolphin to Pandulph)
A Macbeth-like overreaction to a setback; compare #309. But Lewis's loss doesn't even come close to Macbeth's.

NOTES

311. *All's Well That Ends Well* IV.iii.71
(First Lord to Second Lord)
One's virtues cannot be separated from one's vices; it is the combination that makes us who we are as human beings. Without faults, our virtues would grow proud; without virtues, our vices would lead us to despair.

312. *Hamlet* III.i.55 (Hamlet)
An especially difficult question if, like Hamlet, you see "being" as passively suffering at fortune's hands and "not being" as the only way to actively control your fate.

313. *Antony and Cleopatra* V.ii.4 (Cleopatra)
Suicide, the ultimate proof of will, is preferable to a life of humiliation.

314. *Hamlet* III.i.75 (Hamlet)
Contemplating suicide, Hamlet decides that the only reason for living is that death might actually be worse.

315. *Measure for Measure* III.i.128 (Claudio to Isabella)
Claudio repeats Hamlet's theme (#314): Fear of death makes one cling to even the most wretched existence.

316. *Hamlet* V.ii.219 (Hamlet to Horatio)
If God decides when sparrows die, he's surely going to decide when you will die; so why fight it?

317. *Hamlet* V.ii.10 (Hamlet to Horatio)
However we frame our plans, it is a divine power that determines the outcome. Hamlet echoes an earlier speech by

the Player King: "Our thoughts are ours, their ends none of our own" (III.ii.213).

318. *The Merry Wives of Windsor* V.i.3
(Falstaff to Mistress Quickly)
Falstaff refers half-jokingly to the superstition that odd numbers have a mysterious power, especially in matters of birth, luck, and death.

319. *Julius Caesar* II.ii.36 (Caesar to Calphurnia)
The time and place of your death are already determined, so it's useless trying to avoid it.

320. *King Lear* V.ii.9 (Edgar to Gloucester)
Since you can't choose whether or not to die, the important thing is to be ready (*ripe*) for it.

321. *Hamlet* V.ii.336 (Hamlet to Horatio)
Death isn't going to wait around for you to take care of your last-minute business.

322. *Henry IV, Part 2* III.ii.37
(Justice Shallow to Justice Silence)
Shallow didn't need to quote *Psalms* (89:48) to make this fairly obvious point, but he's eager to prove he's well-educated.

323. *Cymbeline* IV.ii.262 (Guiderius, singing)
The rich and famous die like everybody else.

324. *Julius Caesar* II.ii.32 (Caesar to Calphurnia)
Fear of death is itself a kind of death; brave people save themselves for the real thing.

325. *Antony and Cleopatra* V.ii.295 (Cleopatra to Iras's corpse)
When you're weary of life, death becomes a hurt you welcome.

326. *Antony and Cleopatra* I.ii.32 (Charmian to Soothsayer)
Charmian won't outlive Act V.

327. *The Merchant of Venice* V.i.107 (Portia to Nerissa)
Maturity and favorable circumstances bring out the best in things, earning them their just praise.

328. *Hamlet* I.iii.39 (Laertes to Ophelia)
In their youth things are more susceptible to blight and disease. This is Laertes's charming way of warning Ophelia to protect her maidenhood from Hamlet's "assaults."

329. *Henry IV, Part 2* V.v.48 (King Henry V to Falstaff)
Folly is acceptable in youth but grotesque in old age. (Hal, now king, humiliates his old partner in bad behavior.)

330. *Much Ado about Nothing* III.v.33 (Dogberry to Leonato)
Dogberry, the most pompously witless figure in the play, misquotes an old proverb: "When the ale is in, the wit is out."

331. *Love's Labour's Lost* IV.iii.240 (Berowne to King)
Fresh desire makes the old feel young again.

332. *Romeo and Juliet* II.iii.35 (Friar Lawrence to Romeo)
Old people worry about anything, so you expect them not to sleep soundly. But for a young fellow to be up at dawn is odd, as carefree youth ought to sleep long.

333. *Measure for Measure* IV.ii.174 (Duke to Provost)
It's difficult to identify a corpse.

334. *Richard III* III.ii.62 (Catesby to Hastings)
Catesby means dying before preparing one's soul for judgment. Old Hamlet's ghost will complain about this too (*Hamlet* I.v.76).

335. *The Tempest* III.ii.131 (Stephano to Trinculo)
Stephano is babbling, so it's hard to really say what he means, but a likely translation is "Death evens your score with the world," or, more literally, "Your creditors can't get you once you're dead."

336. *All's Well That Ends Well* V.iii.19 (King of France to Lafew)
A banal observation: thinking well of something we've lost makes us recall it more dearly.

337. *Much Ado about Nothing* V.ii.77 (Benedick to Beatrice)
If you don't take care to leave your own mark, people are going to forget you almost as soon as you die. (This includes your spouse.)

338. *Hamlet* III.ii.131 (Hamlet to Ophelia)
Hamlet's cynical comment on how quickly we forget the dead.

339. *Pericles* II.iii.45 (Pericles)
Much as we'd prefer otherwise, we are time's creatures, not its master.

340. *Henry IV, Part 1* V.iv.82 (Hotspur to Prince Henry)
Whether it's philosophically true that time must someday end (*have a stop*), what Hotspur means is that his time is over (the prince has just stabbed him).

341. *King Lear* IV.i.36 (Gloucester to Old Man)
In the finals for Shakespeare's bleakest line.

342. *Hamlet* IV.v.43 (Ophelia to Claudius)
Ophelia's mad, but her ranting does occasionally seem profound. This line has nothing to do with anything else she's saying, but it could mean one of several things, for example: (1) We have no idea what the future holds, or (2) There might be things even we don't know about ourselves.

343. *The Tempest* IV.i.156 (Prospero to Ferdinand)
Life is no more permanent, substantial, or meaningful than a dream.

344. *Julius Caesar* I.ii.18 (Soothsayer to Caesar)
March 15, according to Roman reckoning, and to say the least an unlucky day for Caesar.

345. *Richard III* III.iv.95 (Ratcliffe to Lord Hastings)
Advice from an impatient executioner (*shrift* means "confession").

346. *Romeo and Juliet* IV.ii.6 (Second Servant)
A proverbial quip: if a maker (*cook*) doesn't savor what he makes, it mustn't be very good.

347. *Henry V* II.iv.43 (Dolphin to Constable)
You're better off overestimating a threat than taking it at face value.

348. Sonnet 8, line 2
Sweet things should agree with sweet people, or else something's wrong.

349. *The Taming of the Shrew* I.i.134 (Hortensio to Gremio)
A choice among only bad options isn't much of a choice. (The *rotten apples* at hand are marrying a shrew or getting a daily whipping.)

350. Sonnet 94, line 14
Good things gone bad seem worse than what was bad from the start.

351. *Julius Caesar* IV.iii.203 (Brutus to Cassius)
The trick is knowing which is better beforehand.

352. *Othello* I.iii.204 (Duke to Brabantio)
Moping will get you nothing except more disappointment.

353. *Henry VI, Part 3* IV.viii.7 (Clarence)
Better to deal with threats before they become unmanageable.

354. *The Two Gentlemen of Verona* I.i.2 (Valentine to Proteus)
     Travel expands the mind; staying home dulls it. *Homely*
     here means "simple, unsophisticated."

355. *Cymbeline* III.vi.33 (Belarius to Guiderius)
     If you're really tired, rather than just lazy, you won't com-
     plain about sleeping on stone. A metaphor for the differ-
     ence between hardworking people and spoiled people.

356. *Much Ado about Nothing* III.iii.139 (Conrade to Borachio)
     Fashion quickly makes perfectly good clothes unwearable.

357. *Twelfth Night* V.i.376 (Feste to Malvolio)
     What goes around comes around. In time, which spins
     like a top, your deeds will meet up with you again.

358. *Romeo and Juliet* II.ii.43 (Juliet to Romeo)
     The names we give to things are arbitrary—a rose is a
     rose is a rose, even if we call it a doorknob. Juliet thus at-
     tempts to cancel her and Romeo's surnames, which are
     those of feuding families.

359. *The Merchant of Venice* V.i.102 (Portia to Nerissa)
     Unequal things may seem equally good if you can't com-
     pare them directly. (*When neither is attended* means "When
     each stands on its own.")

360. *The Merchant of Venice* V.i.83 (Lorenzo to Jessica)
     Only the most debased and heartless of men are immune
     to the soothing charms of sweet music.

361. *Henry IV, Part 1* III.i.26 (Hotspur to Glendower)
     Nature isn't all sweetness and light; sometimes it gets sick too, which results in hideous events such as earthquakes. (Glendower has just tried to take credit for a tremor at his birth.)

362. *Othello* IV.i.122 (Othello)
     What's atrocious grammar today was just fine then.

363. *Hamlet* II.ii.303
     (Hamlet to Rosencrantz and Guildenstern)
     You can recognize that human beings are an amazing *piece of work*—the crowning achievement of creation—and still not like them.

364. *The Merchant of Venice* IV.i.47 (Shylock to Duke)
     You can't expect everybody to think and react the way you do—in other words, there's no accounting for tastes. (Shylock's explaining his seemingly irrational demand for a pound of Antonio's flesh.)

365. *Henry V* V.i.58 (Fluellen to Pistol)
     Especially in soups.